For Nicole and Heidi as always.
And for my beautiful grandchildren to be.

My Grandma is an Angel.
She guides me from above.

And each and every single day
she sends me all her love.

She sends me signs to help me
so I know I'm not alone.

Her spirit is all around me.
It always guides me home.

She says if we have faith
then we will begin to see...

That there are Angels everywhere
guiding our hopes and dreams.

My Grandma is in the sunlight
that warms my heart and soul.

I feel her love surround me.
It's everywhere I go.

She's in the stars above me
that guide me through the night.

She's the feeling deep inside of me...
everything will be alright.

I see her in the flowers
that blossom in the spring.

I feel her spirit everywhere.
It's in each and every thing.

She is the graceful butterfly
that flies throughout the sky.

Reminding me that there's no need
to ever say goodbye.

Even though she is in Heaven
we are bound eternally.

Little Bunny Learns How to Be Safe

Ausra Kelley

ISBN: 979-8-815091-46-7
Printed in the United States of America

Book illustrated by Yuriy Speranskiy
Title: Little Bunny Learns How to Be Safe / Ausra Kelley.
Audience: Ages 2-7.

Little Bunny, you're growing up so fast,-
Go ahead and have a blast!
Here are some things you can do every day,
To be sure you're out of danger's way.

Little Bunny, don't you see?
You're about to cross the street.
Little Bunny, don't be lazy.
You must think about your safety.

Peek to the left, and peek to the right.
Make sure there are no cars in sight.
Don't you hop and don't you run-
Crossing streets is not for fun.

Little Bunny, did you know
How hot it is—the fire's glow?
Little Bunny, don't you touch.
It will hurt you, oh so much.

Little Bunny, keep in mind,
There is more danger you can find.
That stove and oven might be hot
Even when there is no pot.

Little Bunny, don't be sad
Did you lose sight of your dad?
Little Bunny, stay in place.
Look around for Daddy's face.

If your daddy's not around,
Maybe help could be found.
Little Bunny, don't you worry.
An officer can help you, surely.

Little Bunny, it's time to play.
Let's enjoy this sunny day.
Jump in the pool! It's fun to do,
But first, make sure it's safe for you.

Ask your mommy. If she says yes,
Then splash in the water and make a mess.
Pool safety is an important thing.
A grown-up and a float are wise to bring.

Little Bunny, if a stranger comes to you,
And offers you a treat or two,
Say "No!" And leave quick!
Don't dare fall for this bad trick!

Little Bunny, if a stranger calls you from their car,
Turn away, and stay where you are.

If they offer you a ride,
"No!" is your best reply!

Little Bunny, what was that ring?
Take good care when the doorbell dings.
Before turning the key in the lock,
Make sure you know the person who knocked.

Little Bunny once you master these rules
You will graduate from safety school!

About author: Ausra Kelley was inspired to write a picture book for children by her son. As a mom of a toddler, she understands the importance of teaching kids about safety. One of her child's preferred methods of learning is reading books. That's when Little Bunny was born. Once she finished writing her book, she realized the value of it and decided to share with others. Ausra Kelley was born in Lithuania, and resides in New Jersey.

Please visit www.littlebunnybarn.com to get updates on Little Bunny books

Made in the USA
Monee, IL
28 April 2025

16506381R00017

For I'll always be a part of her
and she's a part of me.

When I look into the mirror
I see her beautiful face.

When I look inside of me
I feel her courage, strength and grace.

She will always be my Grandma.
This I know for sure.

Her love for me is unconditional.
It's good and true and pure.

She told me that we live on forever
in the hearts of those we love.

And that we are all surrounded
by peace and hope and love.

She is always in my thoughts
and always in my soul.

Her love, trust and faith in me
are the things that make me whole.

So I relax and take a deep breath.
It fills my heart with peace...

To know I have an Angel
watching over me.

Our bond will last forever.
She is always in my heart.

And that is why I know
our souls will never be apart.

Made in the USA
Monee, IL
28 April 2025

16458622R00019